THE SALES~~MAN'~~S ^{person}
LITTLE INSTRUCTION BOOK

THE SALES~~MAN~~'S ^(person's)
LITTLE INSTRUCTION BOOK

Sean McArthur

Thorsons
An Imprint of HarperCollins*Publishers*

Thorsons
An Imprint of HarperCollins*Publishers*
77–85 Fulham Palace Road,
Hammersmith, London W6 8JB

Published by Thorsons 1996
1 3 5 7 9 10 8 6 4 2

A catalogue record for this book
is available from the British Library

ISBN 0 7225 3268 7

Printed in Great Britain by
Caledonian International Book Manufacturing Ltd, Glasgow

INTRODUCTION

If there's one thing I've learned so far in life, it is that you can achieve anything you want if you believe in yourself. If you decide what you really want, and go for it, no one can stop you from getting it.

I have not written this book to impress you, but to impress upon you how much you can accomplish in your life, both personally and professionally.

Selling is a dynamic profession, and I have made it my purpose to learn everything I can about it, by reading books and attending courses and seminars. I have learned, for example, that 80 per cent of business is achieved by 20 per cent of the sales team. If you follow the advice in this little book you can join that 20 per cent.

I've had great fun writing this little book, and I hope that reading it gives you the courage to take that step to Supersales stardom.

Have a great life, and happy selling.

Sean McArthur

ACKNOWLEDGEMENTS

I would like to dedicate this book to my family,
who have given me the space to pursue my ambitions
and reach for my goals.

I would also like to thank everyone at Thorsons,
who have inspired me, both personally
and professionally.

Use your common sense. Most selling is common sense, but common sense is not common.

 Never forget that selling is the lowest paid easy work and the highest paid hard work.

 Keep your eyes and your mind open.

 Love what you do.

Get off to a good start. Leave for work energized, motivated and excited about the day ahead.

 Smile. It breaks down the toughest of prospects. No one has the backbone to stand up to a hearty smile.

 Develop a firm handshake.

Give your business card to everyone you meet, and make sure you get one from them.

 Prepare a polished introduction about yourself.

 Remember, you don't get a second chance to make a first impression.

 Introduce yourself with confidence, and speak with authority and clarity.

When someone asks you how you are doing, always answer positively and enthusiastically. Anything less and they'll wish they hadn't asked.

 Establish a reputation for professionalism in all areas of your life.

 Have belief in yourself, your company and your product.

Don't be embarrassed about being enthusiastic about your product and your company.

 Be dependable and provide a good-quality service.

 Don't compromise on quality. Quality has no substitute.

Don't cut corners. They cut quality, and in the long run they don't save time.

 Don't procrastinate. 'Procrastination is the thief of time.' (Edward Young)

 Strive for excellence in your company and your life.

Refuse to accept anything but the best, and you will very often get it.

 Let your customers know that your product is the best. Most people like to identify with the best.

 Make your customers feel ten-feet tall.

 Never underestimate the value of goodwill.

Form a partnership with each of your customers.

 Never tell customers that they are wrong.

 Don't argue. Arguing never wins an argument.

 Don't moan. Moaning drains energy.

Think well of your customers, and help them to think well of themselves.

 Be sympathetic to your customers. If they need help, offer them solutions.

 Never forget a customer, and never let a customer forget you.

Remember the name of everyone you meet.
If this is difficult, learn methods for improving
your memory.

 Read a book on 'mindmapping'. It will change
the way you learn and retain information.

 Don't just sell to your customers, support
them.

Be kind to your customers. Treat them like friends before you treat them like clients.

 Give your customers a service that is better than they expect.

 Always listen. Poorly paid sales people talk too much and listen too little.

Ask questions. Questions break down barriers and yield valuable information.

 Make frequent eye contact with your customers. Eye contact should be comfortable and direct, not furtive or aggressive.

 Don't speak too quickly. Give yourself time to think. A pause is much better than an 'um' or an 'er'.

Make sure you use the name that your client prefers. If he likes to be called William, for example, don't call him Bill.

 Help customers to visualize a successful future for themselves.

 Give the same treatment to your small accounts as you do to your large accounts.

Make sure you know and understand the purpose and direction of your company.

 Try to serve your customers unselfishly. If you do, you will have very little competition.

 Use a calculator. Prospects will believe in a calculator more than your scribbled arithmetic.

Think of yourself as an extension of your client's organization.

 Work with your customers, as if you're on the same payroll.

 Make it your business to help people prosper in their business.

Understand that the real purpose of your organization is to establish a product or service that enhances the quality of life of the customers you serve.

 Take pride in the quality of your product and the achievements of your company.

 Enjoy your work. Sadly, seven out of ten people don't.

Make sure you know something unique about your product and your company that will excite your prospect.

 Make the effort to find out the history of each client, and record any information you discover about a client, however trivial it may seem.

Want your customers to grow. You can win your customers' trust if you show genuine desire for their success.

 Encourage your customer to tell you about the difficulties involved in his or her business. It will help to build rapport.

Don't be too keen on the sound of your own voice. Remember that a good conversationalist is always a good listener.

 Avoid negotiating over the telephone. The telephone is fine for making appointments; negotiation is best done face to face.

 Always arrive smiling, and leave smiling, regardless of the outcome.

Be trustworthy, reliable and honest with yourself, and everyone you deal with.

 Be scrupulously honest with your expenses.

 Know your product. Excellent product knowledge gives you confidence, which gives your customer confidence.

Don't make promises you cannot keep. And keep every promise you make.

 Dress immaculately and appropriately for every occasion.

 Clear out clothes you haven't worn for a year, and give them to charity.

Be a principled negotiator. Never abandon your values to secure a deal.

 Always look your customer in the eye when he or she is speaking. Be interested in what he or she has to say.

 Keep asking yourself how you can reach more people than ever before, with your excellent product.

'Keep it simple and smile.'

(John Kalench-Kiss Principle)

 Sell your product when your customers want to buy it, not when you want to sell it.

 Always exude confidence and strength of purpose.

If your buyer is insecure, be reassuring and persuasive. Don't bully.

 If your buyer is methodical, be methodical yourself. Go through each step of your presentation carefully and clarify everything.

 If your buyer is a staller, emphasize the importance of acting swiftly.

Remember that you cannot make customers buy, but you can make them want to buy.

 Be aware of body language. A buyer who leans forward towards you is probably very interested in your product.

 Lead and persuade, but don't press and *never* threaten.

Never oversell to your customers. Know when to stop.

 Explain clearly. What we don't understand, we shall never possess.

 Don't make a statement where you can ask a question.

 Learn how to manage your time.

Master the basics. 'Great salespeople, like great athletes and actors, do the basics very well.' (Tom Hopkins)

 Read. Until you start reading and adopt an open mind, you are still serving your apprenticeship.

Before each sale, visualize a successful outcome. Imagine securing the sale. Get enthusiastic about it.

 Do the task you least want to do first, so that it doesn't cloud over your day.

 Be organized and be prepared.

 If you want to get ahead, think ahead.

Define a purpose for every sales call. Know what you want to achieve and write down a detailed description beforehand.

 When you make a visit to a customer, start planning your next one.

 Plan your routes carefully. There's no excuse for getting lost on the way to an appointment.

Never rush to sales appointments. Keep relaxed and focused. Drive carefully.

 Always confirm appointments.

 Plan every meeting in your mind, before you meet your prospect.

 Do the groundwork. Be fully prepared, and have all the necessary paperwork ready.

Focus all your attention on the sale. Don't be distracted from your purpose.

 Don't just talk about the benefits, show them.

 Maintain a positive approach to each sale, and don't dwell on the things opposing your success.

Plan your presentation well. Efficient planning means you spend less time planning and more time selling.

 Take a course in presentation skills or public speaking.

 Try out your presentation as if you were selling to yourself. If it doesn't excite you, you can't expect it to excite your customers.

Make sure that your presentation is professional, smooth, clear and concise. Rehearse well, and check yourself using a tape recorder.

 Whenever possible, have a third party to back up your presentation.

 Get agreement on each part of your presentation before going on to the next.

Repeat your prospect's name frequently throughout your presentation.

 Choose a vocabulary of key words to use in your presentation, ones that your customers want to hear, such as 'discovery', 'easy', 'guarantee', 'safe', 'healthy', 'new', 'tested', 'results' and 'committment'.

Use visual methods of presentation as often as possible. Visuals help customers to remember, and stop them getting bored.

When you present facts about the product, make sure that you also clearly outline the benefits for the prospective customer.

Show that the benefits outweigh the cost of the product.

Find out your buyer's priorities, and structure your presentation accordingly.

 Persuade people, don't manipulate them. There's a fine line between manipulation and persuasion, but manipulation is purely self-serving and persuasion is win-win.

 When presenting, show only the products you want your prospect to buy.

Don't talk to any one customer for more than 30 seconds without a break. Any longer than that, and your prospect will get bored and stop actively listening.

Ask questions that will stimulate the buyer: questions about interests, lifestyle, hobbies and opinions.

Be interested. It will make you more interesting.

 Think of everyone as a potential buyer of your product. You just have to give them the desire to own it.

 Don't waste time with people who clearly have no need for your product.

Remember two of the most important factors for buying: fear of loss and desire for gain.

 Make it the objective of every sales call to help people feel good about you, about the product and about themselves for buying your product.

 Don't forget to sell yourself. It can be just as important as selling your product or service.

Don't forget that your five best friends in selling are 'Who?', 'Where?', 'How?', 'Which?' and 'What?'.

 Prepare a list of open and closed questions. Open questions open possibilities, and closed questions can close sales.

 Avoid the word 'contract'. Replace it with 'agreement' or 'paperwork'.

Don't ask clients to 'sign', ask them to 'OK the paperwork'.

 Use 'yes-tags' – questions to which the only answer is 'Yes'. It's a powerful word: the more you hear it, the more likely you are to reach an agreeable sale.

Listen out for key words and phrases that your client says, and repeat them back to him or her. But be subtle; your objective is to communicate, not irritate.

 Ask a good question and you'll get a good answer.

Avoid talking about the 'cost' or 'price' of your product. Instead refer to its 'value', 'worth' or 'total investment'.

 Try replacing the word 'buy' with 'own' when selling. It puts a different perspective on the situation.

 Never interrupt an objection.

Be wary of the word 'but'. Replace it with 'and', 'however', 'nevertheless' or 'on the other hand' whenever you can.

 Avoid negative vocabulary. Words like 'never', 'can't', 'won't', 'haven't' and 'impossible' only make you feel bad.

Master the art of neurolinguistic programming (NLP). It will add another dimension to your sales skills, and will give you techniques for selling to your customers in the way they want to be sold.

 Feel good about what you say, and what you say will sound good.

 Always have closing forms with you.

Don't object to objections. An objection is just the buyer demanding more information.

 Don't be afraid of being asked challenging questions. Challenging questions should only be a challenge once.

 Learn to love objections. You don't lose to objections, you win by handling them.

Attend business courses regularly.

 Don't be in too much of a hurry to answer a difficult question. A well-timed pause can be impressive.

 Always feed the objection back to your customer. Be constructive: use the objection to gain more information.

Never be afraid to say you don't know the answer to a client's question, but make sure you always find out.

 Never prove your buyers wrong. Praise them for their valid point and overcome their objection.

 Never go for an add-on sale until you've completed the original sale.

Closing any sale is simple. Just ask for the order.

 Don't get complacent. You don't know that you've secured the sale until the customer agrees the paperwork.

 Know more closes than your customers know objections.

 Close with empathy and confidence.

When you ask a closing question, remain silent until the other party speaks.

 When you do secure a sale, reward yourself for all your effort.

 Always apply the win-win principle. Whatever the outcome, make it one that both you and your client are happy with.

If you don't reach agreement on the sale
you originally planned, have an alternative
win-win option.

 Sell benefits, sell needs, sell incentives, and
you will successfully close sales.

 Be ready to close anytime, anywhere.

As soon as one sales appointment is over, look forward to the opportunities that the next one will bring.

 Don't underestimate the importance of recommendation. Referrals come easily when you have a satisfied customer.

 Value your satisfied customers. Satisfied customers buy again.

Never forget that the easiest and most successful business is repeat business from satisfied customers.

 Send every client a letter thanking them for sparing you some of their valuable time.

 After each sale, contact your clients to make sure that they are satisfied with your product.

Learn to become a fine letter writer.

 Keep in touch regularly with all your customers, and they will not forget you when it is time to re-order.

 Listen actively and show that you've been listening.

Keep copies of all letters from satisfied customers, and show the best to your prospects. Satisfied customers are your best tool for prospecting.

 Carry a notebook at all times. Take notes at every opportunity.

Make your reports detailed, interesting and written in a style that is enjoyable to read. Don't ramble.

 When reporting, always offset negative points with a positive statement.

 End all your reports on a constructive note.

Make sure that brochures and new literature are sent out to all your clients regularly.

 Think of yourself as your own distribution company.

 Send a business card with all outgoing mail.

 Advise customers of new trends.

Send all your clients a Christmas card.

 Have pride in what you do, and know you're good at it.

 Take pole position in your sales team and lead by example.

 Develop your self-worth. Value yourself. Realize that you are a special individual.

Be good to yourself. Treat yourself with tender, loving care.

 Join a health club, this week.

 Don't be afraid to be the best in your company. Someone has to be the best. Why not let it be you?

Take the time to eat sensibly. Don't make excuses for eating nothing but junk food.

 Work exceptionally hard at improving and developing your self-image.

 Spend so much time improving yourself that you have no time to criticize others.

 Walk with your head held high.

Don't expect to be perfect. 'If you aim at imperfection, there is some chance of your getting it; whereas if you aim at perfection, there is none.' (Samuel Butler)

 Learn to love yourself. You're the only person you'll be with, all the time, for the rest of your life.

Don't try too hard. Too much effort is stressful. You make more sales with less stress.

 Have a healthy lifestyle. You work at your best when you feel at your best.

 Never look down on anyone.

 Pat yourself on the back – don't wait for others to do it.

'If you want something done well, do it yourself.'
(Benjamin Franklin)

 Don't be a slave to the opinion of others.

 Show respect to others if you want to earn respect.

 Never underestimate yourself. You've probably been doing it for too long already.

'Don't look for heroes. Be one.' (Anthony Robbins)

 Be at peace with yourself.

 Have confidence in your own judgement. 'If you think you can, or think you can't, you're absolutely right.' (Henry Ford)

 Believe that you can achieve each sale, and visualize that it's already yours.

Never turn a sale into a contest of wills.

 Don't criticize, complain or condemn.
Apportioning blame achieves nothing.

 Be positive and direct, never aggressive.

 Don't be afraid of conflict. In today's world,
conflict is a growth industry.

Turn every problem into a challenge, and every challenge into an opportunity.

 Steer clear of controversy. Never talk about politics or religion.

 Be wary of arguments. Arguments can lead to threats. And threats invite counter-threats.

 Keep calm. Never lose your temper.

Make sure that your actions are positive and not damaging. What goes around comes around.

 Be thirsty for information, and pass it on freely to benefit your customers.

 Be generous. The secret to living is giving.

Don't underestimate the importance of reading. 'Miss a meal, but don't miss your reading.' (Jim Rohn)

 Work hard at your job, and work even harder on yourself. 'Make the most of yourself, for that is all there is of you.' (Ralph Waldo Emerson)

 Spend at least as much on the inside of your head as you do on the outside.

Get as much training as you can. The cost of training is high, but the cost of ignorance is usually higher.

 Don't be afraid to be a know-all, but make sure that you never sound like one.

 Remember that the education and development of its employees is a good investment for your company.

Enjoy the learning process. It's great to be good at something, and it's great learning to be good at something.

 Develop a friendly, caring telephone voice.

 Become a tireless researcher.

Answer the telephone on the third ring. Anything less is too eager. Anything more and they might hang up.

 Smile when you dial. Then you'll sound genuinely cheerful when you start to speak.

 Make sure the person on the other end of the phone has a pen and paper, to take notes.

Attend sales meetings with enthusiasm
and optimism. Be open, frank and positive.

 Be meticulous with all your paperwork.

 Keep your desk tidy, so you can concentrate
on one thing at a time.

 Be an efficient planner.

Keep case histories in easy-to-find and easy-to-file order.

 Don't worry about your future; start planning for it.

 Read at least one book on time management.

 'Be wise today; 'tis madness to defer.'
(Edward Young)

Do it now! Think about how good you will feel when it's finished. 'The reward of a thing well done, is to have done it.' (Ralph Waldo Emerson)

 Do one thing at a time, and do it well.

 Do what you have to do as fast as you can and you can do what you want for the rest of your life.

Have the confidence, now, to sell as you've never sold before.

 Be assertive. Learn to say 'no' if you mean it. The other party might not like it, but will respect you for it.

 Believe that you can be the best.

Stretch yourself. The more you stretch the more elastic you'll become.

 Reach for the top. 'When you reach for the top, the air gets thinner, however, the view gets better.' (Andrew J. Reid)

 Be brave. Expect change and welcome it.

Get into the habit of taking one calculated risk daily.

 Aim to become an expert and pioneer in your field.

 Be innovative in all aspects of work.

 Be imaginative. 'Imagination is more powerful than knowledge.' (Albert Einstein)

Relax. You're at your best creatively, when you're relaxed.

 Think laterally. Lateral thinking solves problems.

 'Don't follow trends. Set them.' (Liam Kidd)

 Look for ideas everywhere. Ideas can be found in unexpected places.

Look at something that seems perfect and set about improving it.

 Be patient. Good ideas are not born instantly. They're developed with action.

 Don't be despondent if you have a bad idea. Bad ideas can stimulate good ideas.

If you have an idea, act on it. Ideas only become good ideas when they are acted on.

 Be prepared to look at and do things differently. 'We have to disorganize everything, to release creativity.' (Tom Peters)

 Be optimistic, without losing sight of reality.

Swap leads and ideas with non-competing salespeople. It can generate masses of extra business.

 Set goals. Goals cannot be achieved unless they are set.

 Write out a list of your goals. Putting it in writing makes it a goal, not a dream.

Describe your goals in detail and in a positive way.

 Aim high. 'It is not the mountain we conquer, but ourselves.' (Sir Edmund Hillary)

 Make your goals personal as well as professional.

 Remember, you can turn your goals into reality. This is your chance to write your own script.

Set yourself both short-term and long-term goals. Plan where you'll be tomorrow, and in five years' time.

 Always remember that your ultimate goal in life is to be happy.

 Motivate yourself. Thrive on being a self motivator.

Don't limit your potential. You can achieve anything if you put your mind to it. 'The only limit to our realization of tomorrow will be our doubts of today.' (Franklin D. Roosevelt)

 Practice being confident until it becomes a habit.

Don't let anyone steal your enthusiasm. Energy and enthusiasm towards life give life purpose and meaning. 'Nothing great was ever achieved without enthusiasm.'

(Ralph Waldo Emerson)

 Appreciate the humour of other people, and show your appreciation.

Dare to take risks. Flex your risk muscles regularly.

 But don't be reckless. Look before you leap.

 Rely only on yourself, not on others.

 Think positive thoughts and you will feel positively about yourself.

Cultivate a positive attitude, and your personality will sparkle.

 Combat negativity by repeating positive affirmations. Tell yourself that you are good at what you do.

 Don't be discouraged by the pessimism of others. 'The great pleasure in life is doing what people say you cannot do.' (Walter Bagehot)

Don't blame anyone else if you're not happy. Remember that only you have the power to make yourself enormously happy, beyond belief.

 Always look on the bright side, regardless of circumstance.

 Be grateful to those who offer you help and advice. 'Greater than being great is being grateful.' (Walter Winchell)

Ask for other people's help when you need it. You'll find that people often welcome the chance to give it.

 Focus on the possibilities, not on the impossibilities.

 Concentrate 10 per cent on the problem, and 90 per cent on the solution.

Don't focus on problems all the time. If you do, you'll get them all the time.

 Don't dwell on the past. The past is a faraway country.

 Don't think too much before you act. You can generate fear if you think too much and don't take action.

Don't fail to act because of fear that you'll regret it. People don't regret what they've done as often as they regret what they haven't done.

 Take responsibility for your own thoughts.

 Fear nothing. 'The only thing we have to fear is fear itself.' (Franklin D. Roosevelt)

Have no fear of strangers. A stranger is a friend you haven't met yet.

 Feed your mind with positive thoughts, and you will build positive energy. Positive energy leads to positive experiences.

 Eliminate fear from your life, and replace it with excitement.

Guide your thoughts and direct them towards your destiny.

 Don't wait for miracles. Make one happen.

 Don't ignore gut feelings. Intuition can often point you in the right direction.

 Learn to give 'a little extra' both professionally and personally.

If you want to feel good, do good.

 Give praise and encouragement to everyone around you.

 Get up 30 minutes earlier for work. Rise early and close early.

 Kill boredom by being active.

Make room in your heart for work and put some heart into your work.

 Get hooked on happiness. Being miserable is a habit. Being happy is a habit. The choice is yours!

 Be open to reason.

An effective cure for unhappiness is to go out of your way to help someone.

 Enjoy giving for its own sake, not because of what you might get in return.

 Keep your spirits up. Cheerfulness is a great weapon for fighting frustration, boredom, guilt, envy, and much more.

Be your own best friend.

 'As far as possible, see to everything yourself.'
(Steven Spielberg)

 Take responsibility, now, for what and who
you are.

 Take control of your financial destiny.

Project a powerful image. Try imagining that you have just invested £1 million into the company.

 Don't be uncomfortable with or ashamed of the past. Let it go.

 Be here now. Don't live in the past or the future.

Be prepared to give and take, but give first and take second.

 Be the sort of person about whom people say 'He/she may seem self-seeking and ruthlessly ambitious but he/she has a heart of gold.'

 Never forget someone who does you a good deed. Repay favours as soon as you get the opportunity.

Don't take yourself too seriously. Use your sense of humour appropriately, and as often as possible.

 Be sensitive with your humour, and don't offend. Humour can be a poison as well as a tonic. Laugh with people, not at them.

 'Laugh, and the world laughs with you. Weep, and you weep alone.' (Ella Wheeler Wilcox)

If you want to attract people, make them laugh.

 Accept praise and compliments from people graciously. Few people do.

 Offer your help freely. People want to help people who help them.

 Do it. If you don't do it, it won't happen.

When you take action, put your heart into it – then relax and unwind.

 Look for the good in everyone you meet. 'I always prefer to believe the best of everybody; it saves so much trouble.' (Rudyard Kipling)

 In all areas of your business, be proactive, not just reactive.

Don't vacillate. Make careful decisions and stick to them.

 When you take action, you get results. When you take massive action, you get massive results.

 Remember that you get happiness from life if you put happiness into it.

Reward yourself generously, and regularly.

 Be outgoing. Try to meet all types of people.

 Never pre-judge.

 Think of the day when you can look back on your life knowing that you have given it your all.

Always focus on the good things in life, and how special you are.

 Let go of unhappiness. Only then will you find happiness.

 Don't be an 'if-only' person.

Live today as if it's the rest of your life. 'Somebody should tell us, right at the start of our life, that we are dying. Then we might live life to the limit, every minute of the day. Do it! I say. Whatever you want to do, do it now! There are only so many tomorrows.'

(Michael London)

 Make each day the best you could ever have.

Don't spend all your life thinking about what you want to have, but about what you want to be.

 Never forget, life wasn't meant to be a struggle.

 Remember that life is not a dress rehearsal. You only get one go at it.

 Don't dodge challenges. Tackle them head on.

Don't quit. A winner never quits and a quitter never wins.

 Feel good about yourself and you'll be a magnet to success.

 Accept your failures, but don't make excuses for them. 'We have forty million reasons for failure, but not a single excuse.' (Rudyard Kipling)

Don't work to survive, work to succeed.

 Don't worry about failure. All successful people fail at something at least once in their life.

 'To really succeed and be happy you have to do what you enjoy. Two major principles: I have done what I enjoyed and I believed in my ideas.' (Walt Disney)

Allow yourself to make mistakes. 'The only man who never makes a mistake is the man who never does anything.'

(Theodore Roosevelt)

 Know what you want out of life. The key to success is defining exactly what you want.

Don't be discouraged when things don't turn out as you planned. Think of them as results, not failures. 'Results! Why, man, I have gotten a lot of results. I know several thousand things that won't work.' (Thomas A. Edison)

 Set your sights high. Put yourself in a successful frame of mind.

Don't poison your mind with fear of failure, rejection or disappointment.

 Get into the habit of success.

 Give yourself permission to fail occasionally. Failures and challenges build character.

 Get fit and stay fit. The most successful are the fittest.

Outgrow your 'comfort zone'. You won't grow until you do.

 When you make money, enjoy it. 'Wealth is not his who has it, but his who enjoys it.'
(Benjamin Franklin)

'Recognize, seize and take advantage of market opportunities. Whether you like it or not, there is such a thing as a millionaire mentality.'
(Paul Getty)

 Give yourself permission to get rich. Don't feel guilty about it.

'Empty the coins of your wallet into your mind, and your mind will fill the wallet with gold.'
(Benjamin Franklin)

Think about it. There is no reason why you cannot become rich, if you have an idea that will benefit a lot of people, no matter how simple it is.

Get rid of your money problems, and you'll find that you get rid of most of your problems.

 Enjoy making money, but don't let the acquisition of wealth become your only goal. There are no happy misers.

Love your work and the people you work with.
'If you could only love enough, you would be
the most powerful person in the world.'
(Emmet Fox)

 Take the leap towards financial independence.

 Be determined. With determination, you can
achieve anything.

Find a role model. For inspiration, read autobiographies and biographies of great men and women.

 Believe. 'Believing deeply in something allows all of us to find inner strength and surpass our limitation.' (Soichiro Honda)

'Never give in! Never give in! Never, never, never! In nothing great or small, large or petty – never give in except to convictions of honour and good sense.' (Winston Churchill)

Be persistent. 'Nothing in this world can take the place of persistence. Talent will not; nothing is more common than unsuccessful men of talent. Genius will not – the world is full of educated derelicts. Persistence and determination alone are omnipotent. The slogan 'Press On' has solved and will always solve the problems of the human race.'

(Calvin Coolidge)